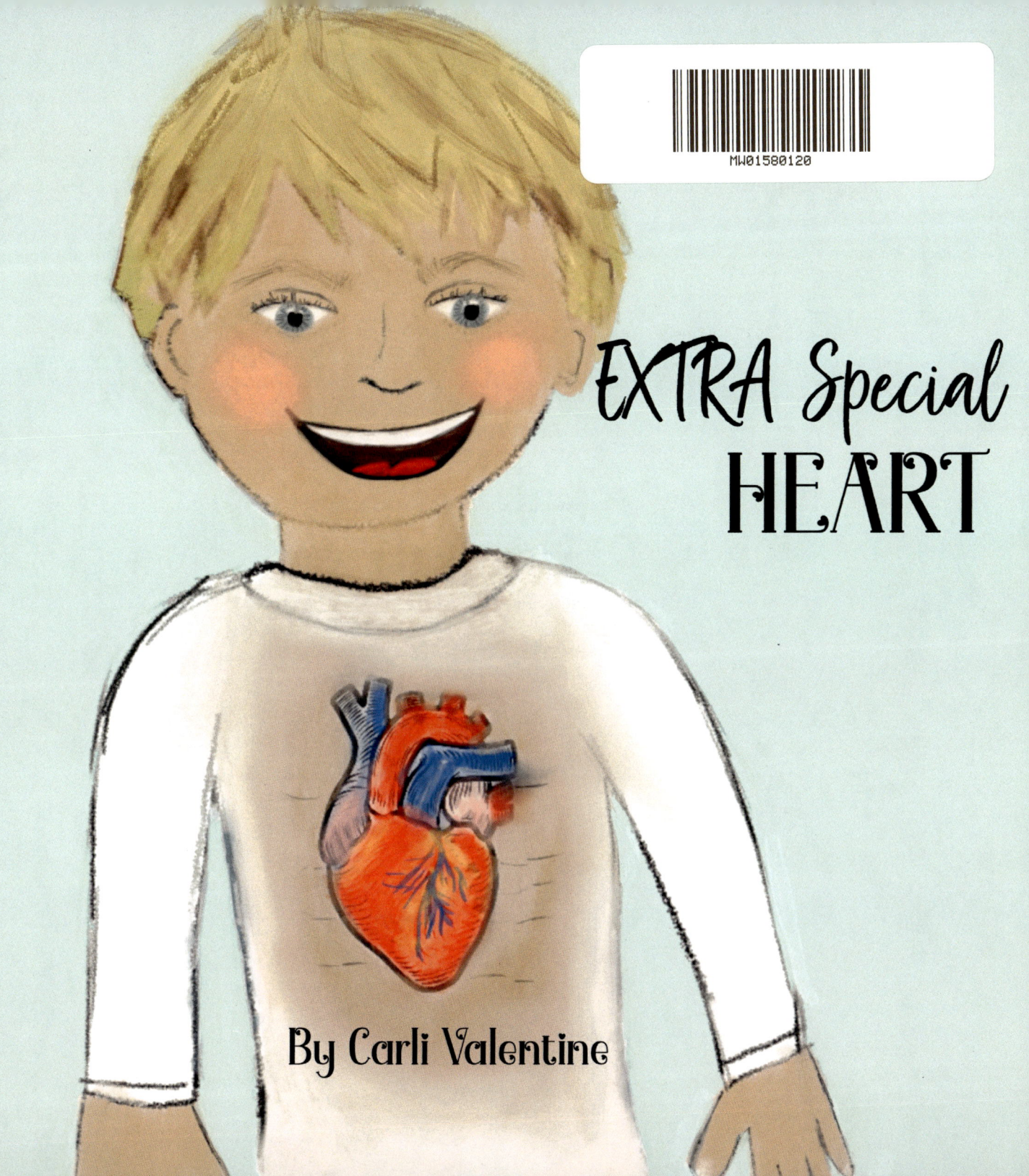

This is a work of fiction. Names, characters, places, and incidents either are the product of the author's imagination or are used fictitiously. Any resemblance to actual persons, living or dead, events, or locales is entirely coincidental.

Text and Illustration Copyright © 2022 Carli Valentine
Book design by Carli Valentine

Published in 2022 by Design By Valentine LLC, in North Ogden, UT, USA. All rights reserved. No part of this book may be reproduced or used in any manner without written permission of the copyright owner except for the use of quotations in a book review. For more information, address: carliavalentine@gmail.com

Library of Congress Control Number:
2022900631

First paperback edition January 2022

Printed and bound in the United States

Book authored and illustrated by Carli Valentine

ISBN (Paperback)- 978-1-957505-02-2
ISBN (Hardcover)- 978-1-957505-03-9

Visit www.carlivalentine.com
Www.instagram.com/carlivalentineauthor
Www.facebook.com/Carli-Valentine-Childrens-Book-AuthorIllustrator-102280112241008/

This book is dedicated to my son, Finn, the strongest, bravest warrior I know! I would also like to dedicate it to all the other CHD (Congenital Heart Defect) heroes with "perfectly, imperfect" hearts.

Photo by Wolf Photography, Utah

February Is American Heart Month and it is vital to spread awareness for CHD research and funding so that improvements can be made. The CDC states that CHDs are the most common birth defect and affect nearly 1% or 40,000 births each year in the United States.

My son, Finnegan, was diagnosed with a CHD called Vascular Ring, in which part of his aorta was wrapped around his trachea and esophagus, making it hard to swallow and breathe properly. He has overcome many struggles and continues to amaze me with his achievements each passing day! Despite numerous trials, he never gives up. His hard work and continued progress is one of the most inspiring things I have ever witnessed.

During our journey, my family has been blessed to meet many other heart heroes and their families. Although faced with very difficult circumstances, they still maintain positive attitudes and share unprecedented love with each other and all those around them.

EXTRA FIERCE! EXTRA MIGHTY...

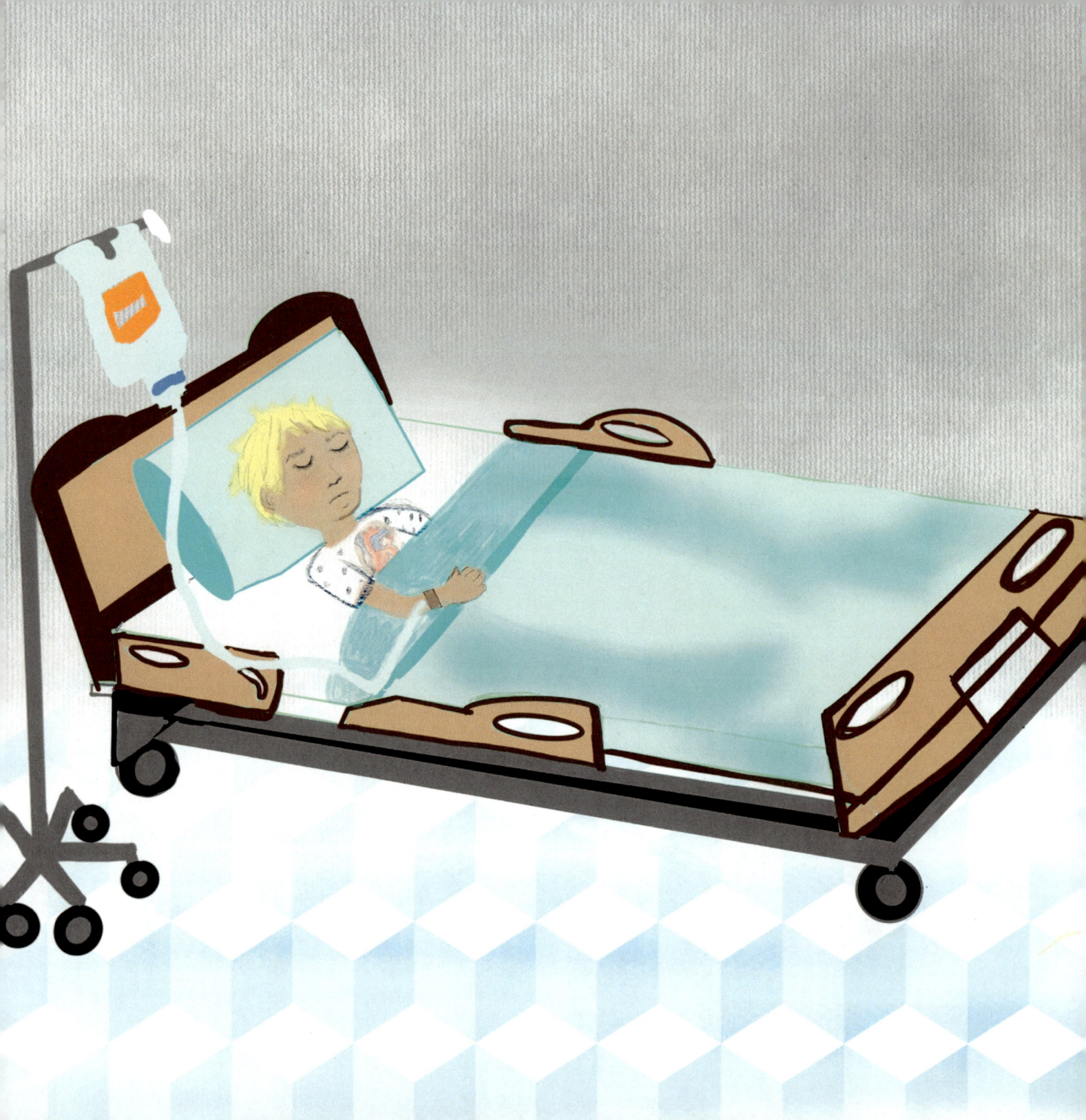

...so it could overcome
VERY HARD things!

GOD definitely put a little **EXTRA** inside, when it was made...

His **HEART** was **VERY SPECIALLY** made!

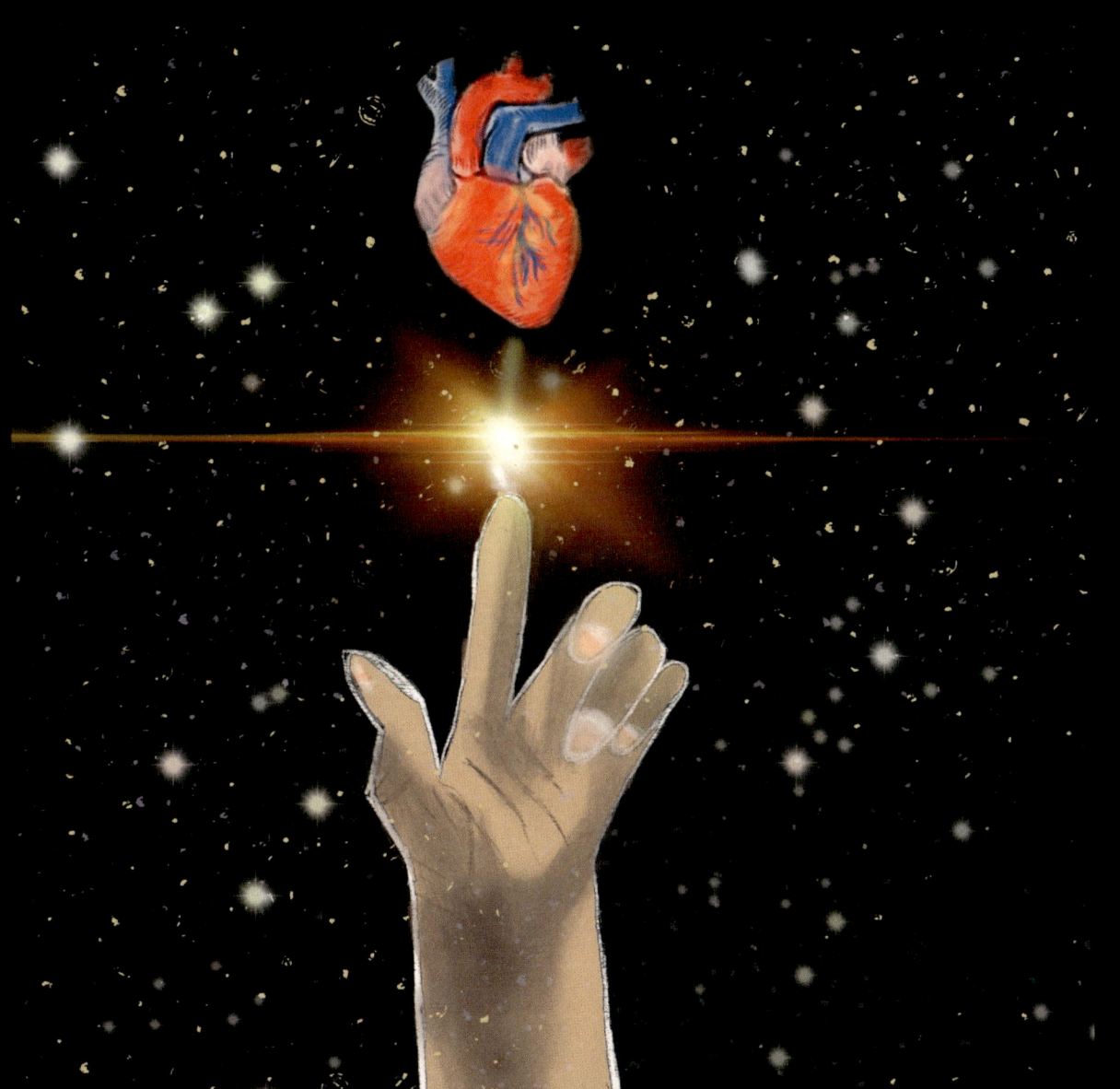

It may have been built **DIFFERENTLY**, and even required **SURGERY** to fix a thing or two. But what was lacking in its **STRUCTURE** and its **ABILITY TO FUNCTION**...

…was made up for with its ability to **LOVE**, both in giving and receiving.

His HEART was built for AMAZING things!

The boy and his heart had overcome many obstacles on a very difficult journey together.

All the **EXTRA STRENGTH** and **EXTRA COURAGE** he was created with helped him to get through many hard situations.

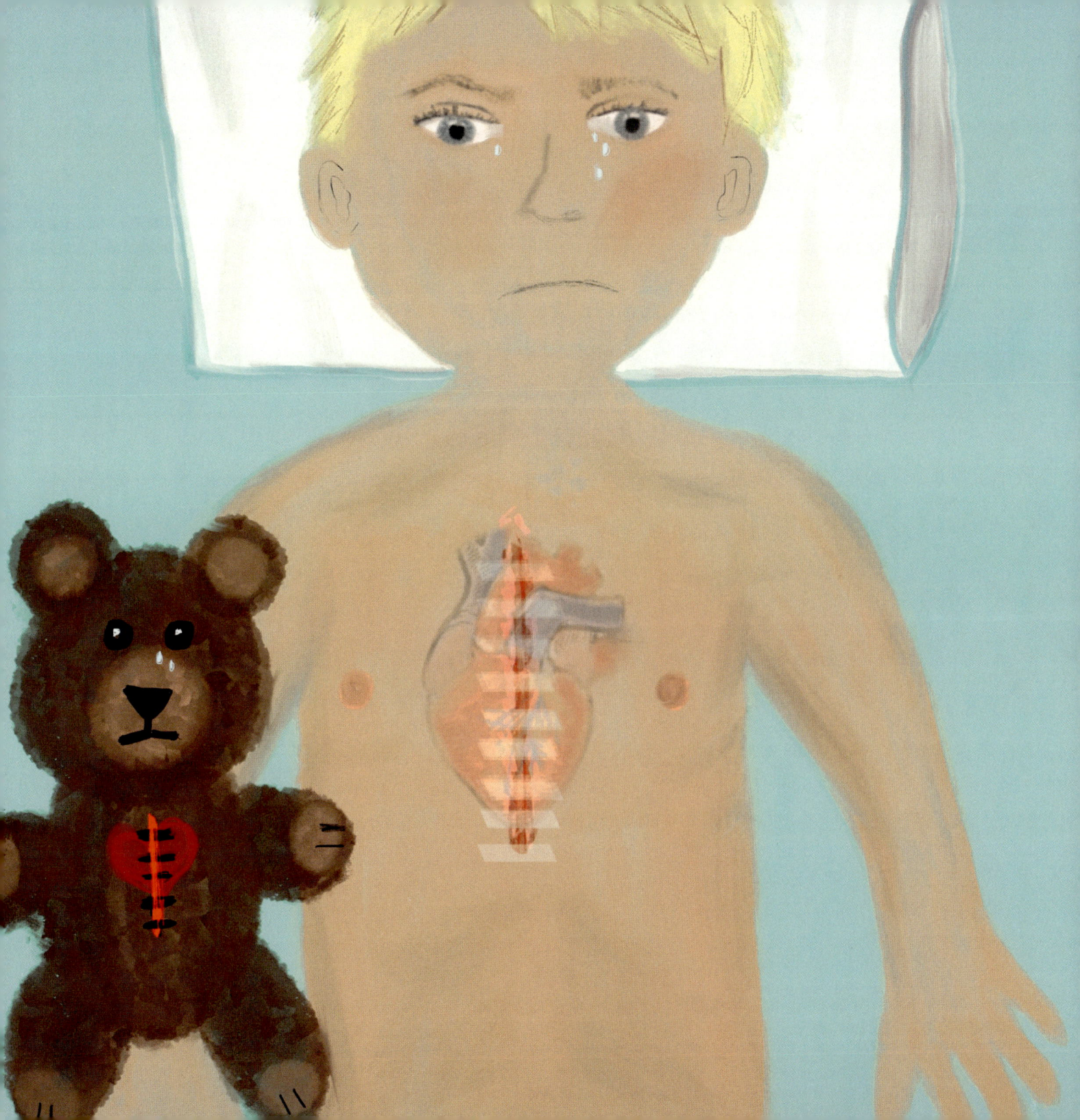

His **HEART** only grew more and more, in **LOVE**, with each challenge it faced.

It was created with so much **EXTRA LOVE**, that he was able to **SHARE** it with others and pass out **SMILES** to everyone he met.

  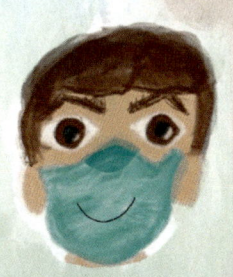 

His **HEART** was created **EXTRA SPECIAL** and the boy was **VERY PROUD** of everything that it helped him to become.

Made in the USA
Las Vegas, NV
16 October 2023